AF595575

I Complete Me

I Complete Me

A Journey to Finding Your Missing Pieces

Sheila Ram Mohan

Notion Press

Old No. 38, New No. 6
McNichols Road, Chetpet
Chennai - 600 031

First Published by Notion Press 2017

PB: 978-1-947202-88-7
HC: 979-8-89519-059-3

For Mom and Dad

You taught me unconditional love

Acknowledgements

The very first book that made me look at life a little differently was *The Power of Positive Thinking* by Dr. Norman Vincent Peale and I have never looked back since then. I believe I owe my positive outlook to this book. I cruised through life – through heartbreaks and debts and criticism, until I met my husband and felt I could let him into my heart and life. Not that the debts and financial struggle went away, but I was content. And then it happened again... two kids, reasonably good life, but I was unfulfilled. And as they say, "When the student is ready, the master appears." My first teacher on this path was Sailaja and her "You can heal your life" workshops. Louise Hay, through Sailaja, changed my life ... and set me on a path that I was never to veer away from.

Feeling empowered with the fact that, like He-Man, I too had power, I then went on to deeper learning. The neuroscience, brainwave therapy and quantum physics culminated in creating a comprehensive easy-to-do journal that you hold in your hands now. Do it once or do it multiple times ... each time, the outcome will be bigger and better and slowly, but surely, you will see the transformation happen.

The list of people I have to thank for making this book possible is long. You don't want to read about them all! This book is shaped by all the books I have ever read, and learned from. I thank my mentors and coaches and teachers – Louise Hay, T. Harv Eker, Gary Douglas & Dain Heer, Erica Marie, Margaret Lynch ... to name a few. The beautiful illustrations in the book are created by my very talented niece, Meghna Menon.

And with deep gratitude, I dedicate this book to my husband Ram Mohan and my children – Vajra and Shourya. But for them, I would not be where I am today. My children, especially, have taken a keen interest to see that I met my book deadlines and that I kept my nose to the grind stone. Even if it meant less home-cooked dinners (yay!) and more takeaways. And my sister, Raji, who has been woken up from sleep, many a time, to hear out my latest chapter or to brainstorm chapter titles.

Prologue

First things first!

There is no documented evidence of what happened to *Cinderella* or *Rapunzel* or *Sleeping Beauty* after they married their respective princes.

And as for me, I personally think *Sleeping Beauty's* Prince Charming was a weirdo, trying to kiss a corpse (well, he didn't know she would wake up, right?).

Cut to modern times: every little girl grows up on fairy tales ... believing that all her troubles will end the moment her Prince finds her.

Bad news: It's not happening to more and more of us.

Good news: Life still continues...

If you have ever been spending your life searching – searching for the right partner, the right body, the right friends, the right place to live, the right life – then this one's for you.

Prologue

My years' worth of quest is what I have put down ... all I can share is what I have learned. You could quickly look at whichever page that catches your attention or you could read it at leisure, but definitely do the tasks. There will be no overnight transformation, but I promise you that you would love the person you become at the end of this book.

Enjoy, my beautiful reader! (Don't look around, I am talking to you☺)

Chapter 1

Let's Start at the Very Beginning

Once upon a time, there was born a little girl, screaming and squalling her arrival. She lived purely on instincts ... demanded food when she was hungry, smiled when she was happy and gurgled approval when she was loved. She was the most divine little creation; everyone admired her beautiful fingers, her ten toes, 'oohed' and 'aahed' when she burped or turned.

You remember that little girl? She was you. Perfection – Perfection in the hairless head, the round food-filled tummy, those chubby cheeks and blue eyes. And then you started growing – watching, hearing, following – and therein started the trouble.

You believed everything you heard, saw or sensed and took it all in without filters. By the time you are a 7-year-old, your blueprint for life has been set. And if you ever act on anything, it is from this framework of reference.

Well, you didn't know any better. Years roll by ...

You have now walked the earth for a fair number of years, and you are still searching for that elusive perfection, that love that will make you feel like the princess you were.

You know what? I found that everything you need is inside you ... you don't need to look outside. And this realization is truly the game changer. You don't need the Big O, you just need the Big G – the big Game.

Social psychologists C. H. Cooley and Han-Joachim Schubert put it beautifully when they summed up what they call the Looking-Glass Self: "I am not what I think I am and I am not what you think I am; I am what I think that you think I am."

The need for approval kills freedom. We are constantly bound by the chains that keep us tied to other people's opinions of us.

So here's the thing.

We create a story of our life ... you heard it right, a story! Like a child who would color with whichever crayon she sees in front of her, we pretty much do the same.

You know the single most frequent line I hear from all the women I work with, "If only I lose some weight, I will find the man of my dreams." This statement comes from most women, regardless of the number on the weighing scale.

The second most frequent line is, "You can do it, you are strong/brave/fearless – add your adjective – but I am not, I have no support."

And it all comes down to what I call the mindset. There are different levels.

We start with the orphan mindset.

"Aaah, Poor me! I am all alone, no one loves me. And they don't love me because I am too dark/ too fair/ too short/ too stupid."

And progress to the martyr mindset.

"This happens only to me, everyone else is happy, and having a rocking time (and by the way, you know this because you have seen their pics on FB). Why me?"

So, let's look at what happens to the "Aah Poor me" state.

Like Linus van Pelt, from the comic strip *Peanuts,* we walk around with this warm, familiar blanket of self-pity – we don't care that it's tattered and torn – we draw it around us and stay buried within our sad stories. We have our own reasons for staying stuck in this victim mode: For some of us, it's the fear of the unfamiliar. For others, they get the attention that they crave. And no matter what, for those few minutes, you become the princess – the one in the limelight again.

And it allows you to stay where you are without rocking the boat.

Let me break it to you.

It doesn't work. Period. I learned this from the mountains.

As I travelled through Leh-Ladakh, I looked at the massive mountainscape all around me and I could hear them in my soul.

Each mountain has its own beauty. I don't think it compares itself to the grey one or the purple one, thinking that its life would be better if it were that lovely brown or that gorgeous green! It stands in its own power – majestic, confident and calm. And neither do we, as observers compare them. I could envision them talking to me about perseverance – no matter how strong the wind, the snow, the rain – the mountains stay grounded; they stay calm and they change and adapt themselves to the conditions, without losing their identity.

And you think the Universe, that made the mountains, would not give you the same awareness?

Chapter 2

Let the Elephants Free

My biggest eye-opener was when I saw how elephants are trained.

When the baby elephants are first brought to work in timber mills, they are tied to a small stake in the ground. The little elephant tries to pull and push, but it's tied too strong. It learns to stay still in that place until his human master commands. The elephant grows bigger and bigger; the stake remains the same, but the elephant does not realize that it could pull once and break free.

We are pretty much like the elephant; we are tied to beliefs which may have worked once, but are no longer true.

Our mind is like the powerful elephant; we can unleash it to create magic in our life or we can tie it to a little stake and force it to live a lie – Force yourself to live smaller, a little weaker and a lot unhappier than you could be.

I always say: The first step to any change is Awareness. So it's time to get off autopilot and start deciding what you want to create in your life.

When we are born, we are born with a clean slate. And then we absorb everything around us like a sponge. The first people we hear and see are our parents. So we begin to talk like them and walk like them and act like them. Make no mistake; our parents, or early caregivers are our heroes. And all our life, we will do things to prove them right. Have you ever been surprised at something that came out of your mouth that caused you to clamp a hand around your mouth and think, "Oops! I sounded just like my mother?"

Then, we start growing up and the circle of those who influences us grows bigger: our teachers, our relatives, neighbors, peers; culture, society, religion, school, media and, because we are such pure sponges, we absorb each and everything without filters and without questions, and that colors our internal landscape. What this also means is that when you are very young, your world revolves around you, so everything that happens, you mostly tend to attribute it to yourself: Let's say you are 5 years old and you hear your mom singing happily and loudly ... you are happy too as you believe your mom's happy because of you. You are 10 years old and your brother and you are cowering under the table ... you can hear your parents yelling and fighting; they seem to be on the verge of divorce. You believe you are the cause. And from here, we pick our beliefs and patterns: *Love equals pain. Nobody loves me. People I love will always abandon me. I will be loved if I please everyone.*

Now imagine this: What would the world look like if you wore pink glasses? And, if you changed them to green? See what I mean?

These things, which we pick from around us, form our thoughts. Attached with our emotions, when these thoughts are repeated over and over again, they become our beliefs. And everything we do, we act based on these beliefs. Don't get me wrong: beliefs are not right or wrong. Our perceptions and our thinking make them so. Some serve us, some don't. A belief that I had while growing up was, "I am always surrounded by helpful people." It is one that has pulled me out of many a pickle.

"I have to work hard for my money" was one such perception I had weeded out in the process because I no longer needed to believe that! Similar to how we upgrade everything in our life, from our laptops to our smart phones, occasionally, we need to take stock of our mind and upgrade it too.

Otherwise, we will become those giant elephants tied to tiny stakes, wearing our green-colored glasses and living our green lives, oblivious to the multi-hued life around us.

Before we go further, there is something you need to understand very clearly.

We are all made of energy: atoms and molecules – that old science lesson which you didn't think was so important! Everything around us is made of energy – the table, the chair, ourselves and our thoughts. And everything is vibrating at its own frequency. Now, your table looks solid, but science tells me that it has the atoms and molecules and a lot of space ... it is moving and vibrating and because you are at a different vibrational level, you cannot walk through it. Thoughts are fine energy and it is said we think over 60,000 thoughts a day. Quite a few of them are repeated thoughts, which become our beliefs and which create our reality.

Your beliefs affect your thoughts, feelings, attitudes and actions and, literally, shape and dictate your reality at a very fundamental level. They are the blueprints and constructs of your world.

To successfully manifest the life you desire, it is essential that your beliefs are in vibrational compatibility with the results you seek.

If, for example, you want a happy, loving relationship but hold negative beliefs about men/women, yourself, relationships, intimacy, commitment, or love itself for that matter, that's what you will create.

Your beliefs are the foundations of your life, and you can't build a dream on faulty foundations.

A few years ago, a movie called *The Secret* – and the book version – created a storm. This movie explained in very simple words about how our thoughts become things, and how, by thinking right, you can manifest all that you want in your life.

Need a cheque to cover house rent? Visualise it.

Want to get into the college of your dreams? Visualise it.

The premise was very simple. Ask. Believe. Receive. Of course, this is what spiritual leaders have been talking about, but suddenly it became mainstream and the "Law of Attraction" became a buzz word.

Now, the Law of Attraction, like all the other Laws of the Universe (Newton's law of gravity is an easy one, remember your old science lesson? ☺, is fail-proof. But it didn't work for quite a few people.

Why?

If it hasn't worked, it's simply because you haven't addressed the underlying beliefs. It's your beliefs that ultimately hold the reins to the boundaries of your experience. It is your beliefs that fuel and direct your thoughts and feelings, and only that which resonates with those feelings can enter your life. If we go back to the previous example where you have asked for the check to cover the rent. You visualise the check coming in, but deep down, you are feeling fear and lack that faith. Guess what will come in to your life? More lack! If you need to change your reality, you need to change your glasses. Otherwise, it's like planting a tomato seed and expecting apples.

So how do you know what your beliefs are? Look at the results in your life. Here's a simple exercise to discover your beliefs:

Set aside some time and ask yourself the following questions. Write down everything that occurs to you as you answer the questions. Don't worry too much at this stage about the whys and wherefores. Simply capture what seems to be the truth to you – pleasant or unpleasant.

- What do you believe about yourself? Write down about 10–15 *I AM* statements. For example, I'm smart; I'm lazy; I'm lovable, etc.
- What do you assume is possible in your life? For example, Life is a struggle; I'll never find love or I always get what I want.

- What do you conclude about other people's relationships in general? For example, people are generally supportive; everyone's out to get me; women are bitches; or men make better friends than lovers ... you get the drift.

Your beliefs will feel really true to you, because you would've had enough experiences to support those beliefs. **Here is something you need to know:** Once you have made up your mind about something, or even someone, it becomes true for you. It becomes your reality. To change your reality, you have to be open to changing your very beliefs.

Let's see how this can be done.

We hold on to our beliefs because there is a pay-off or a reward for holding on to it. Let's see further:

1. Draw two columns. Head the first as 'My beliefs' and the second as 'My payoffs.'
2. Take your original list from the 'Finding Beliefs' exercise and enter all your beliefs for the three questions you asked yourself – both limiting and empowering – into the first column.
3. Consider what your payoffs are for each of those. What does this belief give you? Be specific. Is it a feeling of pride, safety or love? Or is it a very tangible thing such as a great salary, too much stress, or a massive bank overdraft?

My beliefs	My payoffs
I am smart.	*I feel confident that I can hold my own.*
I am lazy.	*I can let myself off the hook.*
I will never lose weight.	*I don't have to try.*
I am lovable.	*I feel secure.*
I can do anything I want.	*I feel powerful.*

If you look around at your friends and loved ones you will see that everyone has their own unique map of the world. All of us see a different version of fact and reality.

Sometimes, simply by recognizing a limiting or disempowering belief, you take away its power.

So, what are disempowering beliefs? Let me give you some examples.

1. I must be perfect in everything I do
2. I must be liked and admired by everyone
3. Disagreement and conflict are a disaster
4. Everyone in my life must be perfect
5. People do not change
6. Other people exist to make us happy and we cannot be happy unless they are
7. People are either good or bad
8. Problems are a sign of weakness and failure

9. People are fragile and must be protected
10. There is only one way of seeing any situation

So, following the earlier thought about "evidence," remember whatever you believe about yourself is probably supported by plenty of evidence. Just changing our assumptions allows us to act differently more often. And create a new reality.

Remember the last time you felt bad about something – angry, resentful, jealous, etc.? What were you telling yourself? What beliefs were behind the self-talk? Thinking about the event, try to fill in this table, writing down any self-talk in your own words. They may include condemnation of yourself and be full of what people 'should' or 'should not' do.

The event: *My best friend forgot my birthday!*

What I felt: *I felt neglected, angry and hurt.*

What I was telling myself: *That nobody really cares for me!*

What it made me do: *Eat the entire chocolate birthday cake fully on my own!*

What my disempowering belief was: *I am not important.*

Here's how you could challenge that self-talk:

Constructive Talk	Feelings Would be	Actions Could Be
Friends really do the best that they can do.	*To feel forgiveness knowing that my friends didn't set out to hurt me intentionally.*	*Recall that other times I had sometimes let them down too!*

In *My Stroke of Insight*, Jill Bolte Taylor states, "We are born with only two fears ... the fear of falling, and the fear of loud noises."

Every other fear is a story that our mind had made up to keep us in our safe zone. The opposite of fear is not courage; it's love. When we act out of love and compassion, we will automatically stop beating ourselves up, or use pitying self-talk. Fear stops you from taking action.

I always remember this quote from Marianne Williamson's book A Return to Love.

"Our deepest fear is not that we are inadequate. Our deepest fear is that we are powerful beyond measure."

How do you feel about this statement? Does it scare you ... or does it empower you?

Chapter 3

Why the Hell Should a Caterpillar Leave Its Cocoon?

All of us who have ever tried to change something know how difficult that task is. My favourite quote that gets bandied around and brings on the "Yeah whatever!" eye-roll on my kids' faces is the famous quote, "Change is the only constant in life."

Have you ever noticed how easy and convenient it is to blame everyone and everybody for everything that is wrong your life? And how often do you stay in the places where you are unhappy, yet don't take steps to change? Ironically, we create a comfort zone around our own miseries.

When I first introduced the concept of "comfort zones" to a group of young adults in a training session, quite a few of them thought that a comfort zone was like eating your comfort food or lying in a hammock. Well, it's not all that soothing. Everything that we are familiar with becomes our comfort zone: the good things such as people we love, the empowering actions we take, the language we use, and the not very good things such as yelling at our parents, fighting with our loved ones; our complaining, our whining or our procrastination. How many people do you know that are holding onto the person they've broken up with 3–4 years ago and are still sad and miserable? Their comfort zone is their victimhood and misery.

How many people do you know that may be holding to the dreams that are way past their sell-by date? Wallowing in failure has become their comfort zone.

And I'm sure, you definitely know someone who is almost decaying by staying in the same job because they feel that there is no other choice? Here, the comfort zone is constantly complaining about how shitty their job is, or how terrible the boss is, and doing nothing to change it.

How many times do you decide to start something new, and the first thing your mind comes up with are the list of reasons as to why you cannot do it?

Our comfort zones become our safe zones, because we know how to do it; the whining, the complaining or the martyrdom.

One of my mentors taught me, *"If you do the things that you have always done, you will get the results that you've always got!"*

So why complain about being out of shape, when you never go to the gym?

Why complain about your job, when you are not willing to step up and step out?

Stop making excuses if you are settling for an unhappy relationship.

Look at one area of your life today: It can be your relationship, your health or your job. Now, here's the time to be totally honest with yourself. Answer these questions:

What do you really, really want?

What are you struggling against?

What have you not achieved yet?

Nothing remains the same. Everything grows. Life is all about movement, and everything grows ... from a blade of grass to an oak tree ... Our inherent nature is to grow into the next level. Anything that stops that growth is against the law of nature. Excuses, justifications and complaints do just that – keeping us stuck where we are.

And the number one reason to why we don't change is because we are expecting the other person, situation or story to change. You remember what I started with: Your beliefs create your reality – Because Life is but a mirror. You can only get that which you give out. If you want to change, scratching that reflection in the mirror does not change anything.

We fear change because we are scared of the unknown. The current situation, no matter how crappy, is familiar to us and we know how to handle it. What if something different comes up? But you know what? Every time you step out of your comfort zone, that zone expands. Remember the first time you learned to walk? You got up, you fell, you crawled again, you got up and walked again ... over and over again, until one day you were walking without even thinking about it. Then you learned to ride the bicycle ... or swim ... or play baseball ... your comfort zone kept expanding.

Everything you want is just out of your comfort zone. The risks of breaking out of your comfort zone isn't nearly as bad as the risks of staying in it your whole life. And that step is necessary for you to grow. Imagine if you had decided to quit walking the first time you fell?

Let me help you with a story. Rita comes to me because she feels overwhelmed by the demands of her family and friends. She feels over-used, under-appreciated and completely taken for granted. So these are the questions I asked her:

What happens every time you tell your "Aah Poor me" story?

What have you made so vital about your story?

Do you think you know it so well?

What would change if you change?

How much courage would you need to stand up?

How would you stop people pleasing?

What would happen if you stopped people pleasing and let yourself be judged and criticized?

How much courage would you require?

What do you think will happen if you learned to respect yourself?

What would happen if you became comfortable with being uncomfortable?

These are the set of questions that you could answer and see what answers you come up with. Again, pick any one area of your life. Think of your life as a story – your story – and write without thinking too much. The first answer that pops into your mind is usually the right one.

You will notice that you usually go through panic and fear at the mere thought, because this is your story and you know it so well ... but as you work through it, you would find some pretty empowering reasons to change.

I have heard that the transition of a caterpillar in to a butterfly is a truly painful process, but it is one that is necessary to transform it from a crawling, fat worm in to a thing of beauty. Anais Nin has very famously said, "*And the day came when the risk to remain tight in a bud was more painful than the risk it took to blossom.*"

That, my friends, in a nutshell, is what change is all about.

Imagine being able to finally be who you are without feeling the need to change, to be liked? Let's face it ... we are mostly worried about what we think other people think of us. They have decided who you are ... it won't matter a smidgen of how you behave after that, as they have already made up their minds. Just be yourself. Because, to quote Dr. Suess, " Those who matter don't mind, and those who mind don't matter."

Now that we have reached here, I want to tell you an interesting secret. Everything you see out there is a reflection of what you have inside you. You simply wouldn't see it if you didn't have it in the first place. In psychology, it's called Projection. So, you like her confidence? You have it. You think she's beautiful? It's your reflection. You think he's a selfish jerk? Sorry to break it to you, darling, but that's you. Anything you want to change has to start from you first. Isn't the thought so liberating?

Like attracts like. And because we are energies, we vibrate at a frequency that will attract other things of the same vibrational frequency. If you are vibrating at the frequency of feeling unloved, you will attract situations and people and experiences that perpetuate the belief that you are unlovable. The only solution is to change your beliefs. Doing the above exercise is one of the ways to do that ... look at why you seem stuck in a situation, and then rewrite it.

Once that happens, because there is a vibrational mismatch, those incidents will no longer come into your circle.

When I was growing up, I had a number of relatives who would criticize me for spending too much time reading – instead of developing 'essential' skills such as cooking and cleaning – for not being smart enough to get married earlier, for being too thin, for being too fat ... I spent a lot of my teen and youth weeping into pillows. It was when I learned about the *Life being a mirror* concept that I realized that the criticism was a direct reflection of my own self-talk. Aah! My favourite topic – Self-talk. Let's discuss further.

Chapter 4

Yes, I Talk to Myself All the Time

The biggest road bump we will face is the conversation we have in our mind or with others about ourselves. Most of us do not even realize the words we use. "I am," as they say, is one of the most powerful words in English language ... and what you tag onto after that creates your reality. I have a special interest in noticing how people describe themselves and their lives. For instance, I have a client, Jane, who says to me, "You know what? I hate talking about money. I am so illiterate when it comes to finances. I just don't understand it. My mind goes blank." And guess what her financial situation is? Complete debt and chaos, even when she is earning well.

Another client Kate is someone who constantly belittles herself, "I am so useless, I am too old. I never understand technology. Smart people have to do more work." It is even depressing to have a conversation with her. And no prizes for guessing where she's at now – For all the people who can see her worth, she walks around feeling miserable, old and useless. She over-compensates by bending herself backwards doing things for others – being over-generous to a fault.

Every word you say or think creates your reality!

So look at what you wrote down earlier. What were you saying about yourself?

I am wonderful. I am loved. I am lonely. I am stupid. I am useless ... You, my friend, are about to take a journey on which you may encounter some dark patches or hit some bumps on the way. Go forth with love and kindness. Make it your intention to love and accept yourself for whom and where you are, right now, irrespective of whatever beliefs you may discover – the beliefs that you hold about yourself and others or the world. Don't beat yourself up because you should have known better, or wish you'd had more empowering beliefs from an earlier date. Remember, the opposite of fear is Love. (Yes, I am challenging your old English classes!☺)

It is possible when you first uncover your old beliefs, you might feel foolish about having lived in such a small box and for having held such limiting beliefs. Be gentle with yourself. You did not know there was another way.

It is time now to let go and move forward. It is time to create a new life founded on new beliefs and venture into the newer zones that you are making.

My intention is to assist you in making positive internal changes and new decisions about who you are and the way life is. Self-acceptance is the place to start.

Before you go any further, it is important to answer these questions:

1. What do you keep telling yourself about life, yourself or others?
2. What kind of statements do you hear yourself making – both internally and externally?

3. What are the thoughts and conversations that run like tape loops in your mind; the ones you wouldn't want anyone else to hear? The ones you wish you could shut out and stop, but seem to come out of nowhere and repeat themselves, whether you like it or not.

Unless we identify the nature and characteristics of our self-talk, it is almost impossible to move forward.

Start doing this on a daily basis. Keep a journal to record and note down your internal and external dialogue.

How do you talk to yourself, about yourself? And how do you talk to friends, family and associates about yourself and areas of your life, or life in general? What do you say about money, your work, your relationships and your children?

Perhaps you hear yourself saying the same phrases or comments that your parents used to make when you were young. What beliefs do these phrases point to? Perhaps, you see similar stories and patterns repeating themselves in your life. Make a list of these statements about how life is, how people behave, why the world is the way it is – the statements you tend to make about yourself, others and the world.

You can stick to an area of life you want to improve or include other areas not there in your self-talk too – be that health, love, happiness, power, work, life, men, women, relationships, sex and so on.

It's a fun-filled and illuminating process. You'll get to know yourself a whole lot more, and the more conscious you are, the more you will be in the driving seat of your life and be able to change its direction, rather than taking the default road.

With a life area in mind that you wish to improve, write down all your thoughts and feelings in free-flow about that area.

Don't hold back, analyze or judge the process; just let your thoughts and feelings spill onto the page. Do this for around 20 minutes. You'll be surprised at what it can reveal – hidden thoughts, feelings, beliefs and agendas can surface.

Once you have written down your free-association, and only after you finish writing, review your notes and the stream of consciousness on the pages before you. See if you can delineate any beliefs there. Look at recurring thoughts, feelings, patterns and statements.

Pick out any faulty nuggets that you wish to discard from your consciousness and write these down on a separate piece of paper that lists your limiting beliefs.

You create your reality with your thoughts, feelings, beliefs, attitudes, choices and decisions, whether you are conscious of that or not. Remember, you can change only that which you are aware of. You are a treasure hunter; every nugget you unearth is a step forward into a newer life.

You have the freedom and ability to change your beliefs, and doing so holds the key to the successes you desire.

It starts with awareness. Taking responsibility for your life without self-judgment or condemnation, though difficult, is both liberating and empowering. New and brighter choices can spring from responsibility. Blame and judgment of others can point to unconscious negative beliefs you hold about others and the world, as well as about you yourself, which you may be projecting onto people out there. Like I mentioned earlier, life is just a mirror, and everything out there is just a reflection of what you feel inside. So a great way to find your beliefs is to look at people and places and situations you have an opinion about.

Think about the traits or behaviors in others that tend to consistently aggravate you, that tend to repeatedly "press your buttons," provoking a strong emotional response. Write them down along with the name of the person.

Then, next to each trait, replace the name of the person who displays that behavior in your reality with 'I am.'

For example:

Donald is pushy and aggressive ... I am pushy and aggressive.

Jane is so arrogant ...I am so arrogant.

Karen is a liar ... I am a liar.

Henry is cold and unresponsive ... I am cold and unresponsive.

You may find that when you write down the 'I am ...' statements you might recollect memories or situations when you have, either to yourself or another, acted or thought in a way that corresponds with the trait, behavior or attitude that you are judging in the other.

The person who has the trait you dislike in your world could be a mirror - magnifying the quality that you may be denying in yourself, and bringing it to light to acknowledge, forgive and change.

You may dislike people that are judgmental to others, yet you may be judgmental to yourself. For example, I have often stated emphatically, "I hate liars, I hate deceit." Until it dawned on me that there were certain areas in my life, where I was lying to myself, where I was not being totally honest with myself. Once I uncovered this and stopped, I found that I was attracting more and more honest people into my life. This exercise is a way of working with your shadow – repressed self-beliefs and negative self-concepts that can be hidden from conscious awareness and projected onto the world.

Now, I am not suggesting for a moment that you are like that all the time. Don't make the mistake of identifying with your shadow and feeling guilt, besides having self-attack or judgment/condemnation. There may be areas in your life where you may have behaved like that. It does not mean you are made only of these qualities. You are not only your darkness, failings or mistakes. Neither are you always pure and snow white. It is uncovering the dark and the light within you that sets you on the journey into achieving wholeness.

People, in reality, reflect your beliefs through their actions and words. And, unless you get to the heart of this, you will continually attract people who have the same traits, or patterns – be it a new boss, your partner, your friends or your children.

And as you address, heal and change the beliefs that lie at their roots, your life starts to change and the people that surround you also start changing, stop bothering you or move away from your life. Another way to do this is to write down judgments you may have about various subjects:

Men are...

Women are...

Bosses are...

Money is...

Rich people are...

This may seem like a simple technique, yet it can be highly effective. I have had some powerful revelations with this technique and have identified inner beliefs that I was blind to and had not been revealed to me through other processes.

You want to identify the most fundamental limiting beliefs as these are the ones that will be having the most impact on your life and glue the related constructive thoughts and feelings in place. Most core beliefs are usually "I am not good enough" or "I am not lovable enough." This is like pulling out the weeds of unwanted thoughts completely from the garden of your mind, so that no more such roots exist. The entire belief plant dies. Otherwise, you would just be cutting off the top leaves and the plant would still be growing and manifesting itself in your life over and over again. One way to aid yourself in recognizing the most fundamental beliefs is simply by the depth of the feelings they trigger when you read them, say them out loud, or think about them.

You often know when you've hit a 'biggy' by the internal dial of your senses – your gut feeling – by the depth of feeling it triggers inside.

When something happens in your world, for example, an event or circumstance that causes you to react or triggers strong emotions, look at the button that is being pressed internally.

What is the hotspot – triggering factor – of emotion at the heart of your reaction? If you could describe in a few words what really bugs/hurts/frustrates/enrages/scares you, write that down.

Let me give you an example: Clara has been separated from her husband for 5 years. They have a daughter, Emily. Now that Emily is almost an adult, Clara and John signed the divorce papers and everything's amicable. The divorce came through easily enough. Then, Clara hears that John is getting married again – to the woman he's been living with and who Clara knew about, had met and really liked. John does not tell Clara that he's getting married, (we will dwell about those reasons later, and no, 'he's a jerk' is the wrong answer). He invites everyone, including his daughter, to the wedding. Clara is devastated. Does she want him to get married and move on? Of course, yes. Is she happy for him? Resounding Yes. What is the issue? The fact that he is getting married, but did not tell her had brought up the feelings of "I am dispensable" – the twin sister of the belief, "I am not good enough." That was her red hot button.

So, what's yours? Find out the pattern that you keep repeating in your life which triggers those emotions.

Often, what you try to prove to the world can be a sign of an opposite belief you are defending against. For example, if you are always trying to be over-generous to a fault, a people pleaser, perhaps deep down you believe you are bad, wrong or not good enough.

If you are overly independent and strive to do everything yourself, perhaps you are defending against a needy dependent self that you think of as being weak.

If you are a perfectionist, perhaps you are compensating for shame and inadequacy and a belief you are faulty or flawed.

It is the beliefs that we are least conscious of that we tend to project onto others, so these exercises can help with bringing them to light.

Once you finish this exercise, also remember that beliefs are not right or wrong. We are just clearing out the closets of our mind, so that there is space for more empowering beliefs. And you could not have done this a minute earlier. This is the right time. This is the right place.

Chapter 5

Unchained Melodies

Here I am, sitting on the banks of the lovely turquoise Indus River, and I know this song ... it is teaching me how to go with the flow. I see it often in the simple things of life ... like when I try to pull open a closed door, I end up getting frustrated and panicky – depending on whether I am in my bedroom or in my bathroom ☺ – and then I notice that all I need to do was turn the handle gently to open the door.

Life is that simple and easy ... really! We make it complicated with our thoughts, our expectations, our conclusions and our illusions.

So, learn from the river ... watch how it flows over the rocks, around the logs, washing itself off all baggage. Always clear of resentments ... skipping along.

So here's what we don't realize ... we are all made of the expectations of what we think others would like to see in us. What we think would make us okay and fit in. So we dim our lights, turn off the parts that we consider may not fit in, and squeeze ourselves into shells to be accepted. It happens in most relationships.

You know, if you met me now, you would say that I am powerful, positive and clear about what I want and how I want what I want. I know because I have people writing to me or saying that they would have to really learn to be like me. Well, I wasn't always like this.

I never spoke out of turn; I was too sensitive to what the other person was feeling, and how I would be perceived. I thought my biggest job was to maintain status quo in all relationships, and avoid confrontation at all costs. So I would swallow my angry words, mute my mouth and pretend all was well. And emotions not expressed in one way, tend to show up as road rage, anger towards my children and a skin riddled with allergies. By the way, skin health has a lot to do with your individuality, so every time you find your individuality threatened, you will develop skin-related health issues. And in order to gain acceptance, I kept changing myself to suit the other person. You know how this ends right?

I realized that when I live in a space of authenticity and freedom, I actually give the other person freedom to be who they are. Of course, some people may leave you, but that's okay. Because the people who are left in your life are the ones who accept you as you are.

I am not saying it's easy. It's definitely not easy to turn off years of conditioning and patterns. Once you identify your beliefs, your payoffs and the life you want to create, it's time to let go ... of all that is weighing you down, all that does not serve you.

So what are the various reasons why we shrink ourselves, play small and people please?

Have you heard the old nursery rhyme, "Girls are made of sugar and spice and all things nice?" That has been ingrained into our DNA ... as women, we are supposed to be sweet and gentle and kind ... I am not saying that's a bad thing. But to be sweet, when you want to scream your head off, to be sweet just because you are scared you won't be liked, to be sweet when all you want to do is go loping off to find the toads ... that just results in us stuffing our anger, creating drama in our bodies and playing with our health. What's with the weight issues that hit most women? Because we don't find an appropriate outlet for our anger, our anxiety and our insecurities, we turn to food. Add to that our bitching about our lives to our "close" friends; it's a sure fire recipe for more shit in your life. And, what you focus on grows ... so the problems you are focusing on might just seem to grow and grow and never change.

Trust me on this one: when you stop obsessing about being more lovable and likeable, you will actually attract more love in your life.

The other reason we people please is because we have never been taught to set boundaries and say *no.* We were taught that it's important to put others before you, or else you were labelled as "selfish" and self-centred." As you go through your day, feeling the weight of your own boundary-less life, you start developing the martyr mentality. Somehow, suddenly the 'poor me' mind set becomes a much stronger drug that keeps you steeped in martyrdom. Which is why you have so many women staying in abusive relationships, and holding on to the belief that "at least he or she provides for me, or cares for the children" or one of the equally foolish reasons. Make no mistake; we teach others how to treat us.

And every time we accept abuse – physical or emotional – we are killing smaller pieces of ourselves such that at the end of it all, we are much smaller and more lost.

Setting boundaries helps you retain the love for yourself, so that you have more to give others. Tell me, how will you give to others that which you do not possess yourself?

We are creatures of duality: we have the bitch in us; we have the goddess in us. So when you drop your façade and your fear of what other people might think of you, you will give and receive from a space of genuine love. People pleasing has its roots in fear: fear of losing other people's love. You don't need to earn that love. You are lovable because you are! So let go of the sweetness and malleability and settling down. Stand up. Like the river, let your energies move freely and lightly. And when you start loving yourself, you reflect that love out in to the world and get it back, many times multiplied.

If someone gives you a hard time and says, "You've changed," it's not a bad thing. It just means you stopped living your life their way. Shrug and move on ... and you have given permission to the entire sisterhood to be who they truly are – powerful, authentic and genuinely loving.

Because they choose to, and not because they have to.

Task:

What are you ready to release from your life?

What patterns? Which beliefs, people or situations are you holding on to that's creating this misery in your life?

Chapter 6

So What the Hell is Self-Love?

My life took a 180-degree turn when I learned this concept: We can only be loved to the extent that we love ourselves. And it created a tremendous shift in my personal, professional and spiritual life.

How do you know if you aren't loving yourself?

You constantly criticize yourself, your body, your hair, your abilities and belittle everything you do. You talk about yourself in less than flattering ways – and pretend it's because you want to appear humble. You refuse to set boundaries; you never know how to say NO.

We are never happy in our relationships or in our life. We are constantly doubting ourselves when people compliment us.

The self-doubt: *Are they secretly laughing at me or are they saying it just to make me happy?*

Do they call us when they said they would, after the first date?

The self-doubt: *If they didn't, is it because I am not interesting enough?*

Do they initiate sex, or cuddle like they used to, or hold our hands when we walked down the street?

The self-doubt: *They are losing interest. They've met someone else. May be I'm less desirable than I was ten years ago.*

We don't trust our partners.

We think they are cheating. *Where was he last night? Why didn't he pick up the phone when I called? Why was his other phone busy for so long?*

The self-doubt: *Am I not good enough? I look old!*

By the way, I have even heard 24-year-olds say, "Oh my god! I am old, maybe he's with a younger woman!"

We'll always be looking for evidence that they are secretly losing interest. We can't tell them our secret feelings or fears, because it will push them away. We feel like we "aren't good enough" to date our crush, or we settle for someone who is "safe" or "fine," but who doesn't make our heart leap with joy.

We carry around the pain of never feeling good enough to have the kind of love that other people experience. We doubt ourselves; we doubt our partners; we doubt love. And in a bid to retain that love, or even worse, to earn that love, we won't set limits and boundaries and let people walk all over us.

We won't ask for a raise; we'll stay in dead-end jobs. We are afraid to charge a decent amount for our services. We procrastinate over things that need to be done.

We create illnesses in our body. We give up on our self-care and become harassed, harried, unhappy versions of ourselves.

We'll look for quick fixes to make ourselves feel better: a new haircut, a one-night stand, a bottle of whiskey, an ice cream tub, or shopping sprees.

But none of these fixes fix us at all. They leave us feeling lonelier, emptier and sadder. And we will remain that way **until we stop looking for other people to give us the love and care we yearn for and deserve.** We do whatever we can to avoid looking inward, because looking inward feels scary. We will do whatever we can to avoid acknowledging how we feel inside. Remember the times you have felt the need to constantly be busy? So that you don't find the time to look at what's happening in your life?

But we are wrong ... so very wrong about what loving ourselves means, and how it feels.

After all, why would someone else love us, if we don't think we are worthy enough?

Here's the thing about loving ourselves: until we do it, we don't realize its power.

We think the reason for our unhappiness is "out there," and we go around searching for someone, or something, to solve it for us. We reject self-love as the powerful, uplifting force in our lives it can be. We buy into the belief that it a concept for delusional people, and that it is ridiculous.

The first commandment about loving yourself is to stop all criticism. This is something I learned from Louise L Hay's *You Can Heal Your Life* workshop that was the stepping stone in my journey of self-actualisation. The proof of loving yourself is finally showing up as who you really are. And accepting yourself for who you are. You speak *your* truth and ask for what you want.

You **don't need to prove anything** to anyone, because you know the only opinion that matters about your self-worth is your own.

Remove all the "should dos" from your life and system. Don't **accept bad treatment**, or social pressure, or feel compelled to do things you don't want to do just because you are "supposed to."

You **aren't afraid of getting hurt**. You don't push love away, or run away, or subconsciously create reasons as to why your relationship would let you down. You let go of all baggage in your life: people, situations or things that are causing the drama and trauma in your life.

When you finally start loving yourself, you can channel that energy into creating a life that you love.

Task:

Here you go: two small tasks to practice loving yourself.

1. Look in the mirror, look into your eyes and say "I love you" to yourself.

   For most people, the idea of telling themselves "I love you" as they look at themselves in the mirror is a tricky exercise. The thought of doing so can feel awkward or silly. It's just not an easy thing to do. In fact, for several days after my workshop, I intended to practice Louise's suggestion, but I kept forgetting about it. Then, one night before going to bed, I was washing my face when I remembered my intention. Finally, with the mirror in full view, I looked into my eyes and said, "I love you, Sheila." Immediately, I felt self-conscious, as if someone were watching. I tried it again and glanced away, feeling embarrassed. On my third attempt, I found myself focusing on the wrinkles around my eyes, the hairs that needed to be plucked at the edges of my brows, and the way my skin seemed to sag a bit at my throat. Great, I thought. *My attempt at self-love has now turned into a critical assessment of my aging process.* I was failing miserably. I've come a long way since then ... now I can look myself unabashedly in the eye, blow a kiss and say "I am awesome." And my life reflects that! ☺

2. Every day, write down two good things about yourself. It can be as simple as sharing a smile with someone, or cleaning your closet or as big as a huge account that you won, or a client you signed up. Praise your hair, your skin, your style or that your dog wagged his tail when he saw you... I don't care ... remember that for flowers to blossom in your garden, you don't pour scalding hot water of criticism. You water it with praises, affirmations and nurture it with gentleness, compassion and love.

Chapter 7

Finding Those Missing Pieces

I Complete Me

When my daughter was very little, during one of our meanderings in a book store, we picked up a book with huge print and funny cartoonish drawings. It was called *The Missing Piece Meets the Big O.*

As with all children's book, the messages are not just for the kids, it is a profound message for adults. Silverstein tells the tale of a lonely little wedge that dreams of finding a big circle into which it can fit, so that together, they can roll and go somewhere. All of us, who have waited or are waiting for our Mr Perfect to roll up and sweep us into his arms or Porsche or his fairy tale life, will identify with that.

Partly, the stories we are brought up on are to blame. No one ever has written a sequel to your *Cinderella* or *Sleeping Beauty.* Most relationships do not work because we are getting into it with a false premise. True love doesn't complete you. It helps you grow and become more of what you are truly meant to be.

I used to go all mushy and starry-eyed when I watched movies where the hero holds the hand of the heroine and declares, "You complete me." Remember the line from *Jerry Maguire* where when he says, "You complete me," she says, "You had me at hello." In reality, all relationships will be wonderful if we are like Drew Barrymore in 50 First Dates. Every day, she wakes up with no memory of the previous day and has to go through the tapes to remember the people she has met. How cool is that?

Most of the time, our need to fit in is so strong that we will cut ourselves into pieces and shut off parts just so we fill the mould of "being okay." We constantly assume ourselves to be wrong. For example, let's say your partner feels there is something wrong with his life. You immediately assume that it is you ... So, you try to fix the situation by seeing which parts of you need to be turned off. Constantly judging ourselves, criticizing ourselves and compromising on what we love, we slowly divorce parts of ourselves to be in the relationship. I should know; I've been there. I look back at my life and I see the times when I should have spoken up and I didn't, because speaking up would have marked me as "different." I see the number of times I went to a party I didn't want to go. I wore a dress that I didn't like or ate food that disgusted me because to not do so was, "unacceptable." I remember the friends I had let go, the hobbies I had given up, the convictions that I had held closely to myself because I didn't want to rock the boat.

So often, when our partner says they don't like our work place or our colleagues, we give up on them. He says he doesn't like the clothes we wear, the words we speak, the tone of our voice, the way we walk, the way we cook ... We try to change everything.

See, the fact is that our partner falls in love with what we show them in the beginning of the relationship. Then, slowly we change, and then we wonder why our partner doesn't seem to like us anymore.

With every criticism, we keep trying to change and fit, hide and fold ourselves into what we think is a more lovable version of ourselves. And as we keep shutting off parts of ourselves, we keep dimming our own light and living in misery, believing that this is the way to true love.

Have you noticed that in order for people to be a 'couple,' they are constantly questioning whether it's okay for them to be this or that because they are a couple. You spend your entire life trying to prove that your choice of that person is right. Louise Hay very famously asks, "Do you want to be right or do you want to be happy?" To be truly happy, you have to be willing to accept that you can be wrong.

While this true for a lot of women, I am seeing a lot more heart-centred men also go through this drama of changing to keep the partner. And you think it's worth it?

The fact is that we are constantly changing. We are not the same person we were yesterday. We will not be the same person tomorrow. That is why it is truly unique to have a person who is willing to let you be that and allow that change. But because we are afraid to change, we try to stay in the same box where we think the other person wants us to stay. And then, we wonder where we lost our mojo!

True love is not about adjusting and shutting off. True love is about supporting, contributing, nurturing and growing. Partners who are willing to constantly change with each other have an amazing relationship. They help each other expand their limits, and become truly more of what they can be. They don't try to manipulate or control the other out of the insecurity that he or she will go away and find another. In fact, when you try to get somebody *not* to leave you, the person who leaves is you. Gary Douglas has said that! What a powerful statement.

All of us operate at the level of energy – in terms of our molecules and their vibrational compatibility. You remember that, right? And we can never have anything which is not in vibrational compatibility with us. Every thought you think, manifests into a tangible form. So, if you are going in to a relationship by cutting off, shrinking and hiding, guess what you will bring in to existence? A smaller, messier and more incomplete relationship.

There are two levels that we operate from. One is the Victim Mode, where everything happens to you. You believe you do not deserve love, so you attract abusive relationships. Yet so strong is your identity with your victimhood that you stay on, making excuses and stories for their behavior. Or you are in a Saviour Mode, where you believe you have to save the other person. You believe that you are the more evolved person and if you leave the relationship, your partner may not survive. Here also, you have excuses and justifications for how you are responsible for your partner's flaws and bad behavior. He/she is suicidal; your leaving will kill them; the kids need you to be together, no matter how dysfunctional ... or even, your parents would not be able to handle your divorce ... the reasons are endless. I've heard them all.

Here is where I want to introduce you to the concept of allowance or allowing – where you include everything and judge nothing. Allowance means being willing to let things be as they are with no point of view about it. Nothing is good or bad or right or wrong. It just is. Just be aware of its existence.

Now, allowance is not acceptance. Acceptance is when you believe, "This is how it is, and there is nothing I can do about it." Or you resist and react to it. Either way, it is a judgment that locks you in. Allowance, on the other hand, is knowing that everything anyone else may say is just a point of view and has no connection to you. You don't have to agree and align or resist and react.

It is different from tolerance or patience. Tolerance is 'putting up with.' Let's say you disapprove of smoking and your partner smokes and drinks. Tolerance is when you let your partner continue doing it even though you are not happy about it. You are agreeing to suffer in silence.

Patience is waiting for someone or something to change. You are putting your life on hold until it changes. For instance, you wait for your partner to realize that smoking is bad, and all the while, you have judgments: smoking is bad; my partner has no will power; he has no good stress buster habits or what is he teaching our children?

If you are always fighting for or against, you are exhibiting polarity – the either/or version. When you are locked within the polarities of right and wrong, you have no choice.

To be in allowance is to acknowledge your partner's choice and be willing to choose for yourself. When you are in allowance, you will tell your partner, "I hate it that you smoke and drink and I am not willing to put up with it. You can do whatever you want, but just don't do it around me or in the house." This immediately creates a space for change which may happen or may not happen. But you have to move yourself from the position of a bystander to the main character and include yourself – what you like and what you do not. Allowance is an "interesting point of view" without any judgment.

There is no right or wrong; it just is. When there is judgment, there can be no love or no relationship. And that is when you create unhappiness for yourself.

And because our reality is but a reflection of what we are, when we are in allowance, we will also give ourselves the permission to gather all the pieces of ourselves that we have hidden, given up, modified, folded or discarded. We look at ourselves without judgment. Everything that we notice about ourselves is just an interesting point of view. And that's when true change starts to happen. That is when we finally allow ourselves to shine with the full recognition of our own powers and be all that and more of what we truly are. And who knows, when you do that, you might inspire others to do the same, who might inspire a few others. And that is how the planet changes.

When you are whole and complete within yourself, and in complete allowance and approval of who you are, you will attract a partner – if that's what you want – who himself or herself is complete, who wants to contribute to your growth and also wants to help you push to your edges and fly, while they keep pace with you.

So here's a task for you.

Be aware of your choices. And how do you do this? By asking the right questions. No matter what question you ask, your mind will scramble around to find the right experiences to answer your question. So asking yourself, "Why is my life so crappy? Or why are my relationships so wrong?" will keep you in the gutter. Quit overanalysing. Just ask, "How does it get any better than this?" And remember to ask the question frequently to yourself. Wait for the experiences to appear. When you ask that question, you are asking for the vibrational energy of how to make something get better, and that in turn, allows for possibilities to show up.

Chapter 8

Sweetening the Deal

Mary Engelbreit says, "Don't look back, you are not going there." The past is over and no amount of time travel in your mind can change what has happened. I always believed that fairy tales actually hold great life lessons for us adults too. Alice is my favourite fictional character, growing up...and even now. What a chick! Jumping down rabbit holes, eating, drinking whatever she sees, living life on the edge – with no thought about consequences – saying what she means, and "She means what she says!"... She is my hero! One thing that she says has stuck in my mind all these years, "It's no use going back to yesterday, because I was a different person then."

Truth! Your experiences have shaped you to be who you are. Your present is the sum total of the thoughts you "had thinked" and the actions you did. Now if you want a new future, you have to see what thoughts you would like to keep and what you would like to change. Sometimes, we wish we had a magic wand, right? And that we could Harry Potter our way into everything that's magical.

What if I told you that I can give you not one, but two such wands?

Forgiveness and Gratitude: These are two beauties that I keep in my spiritual tool shed.

Let's start with Forgiveness, which is a red hot button for most people. Having read about how you have created your life may bring in self-blame and anger. And, in many cases, we immediately proceed into our stories of victimhood and martyrdom. I don't mean to diss you or your feelings, but here are the most common lies we tell ourselves about forgiveness.

- **Lie no 1:** Forgiveness is for the other person. In truth, we are not forgiving the other person; we are giving ourselves the permission to release the chains that bind us to that story. We are letting ourselves move into freedom. This is true of self-forgiveness too. Often, we are the harshest on ourselves and remain tied to our old stories ...We believe we deserve to be "punished" or we "deserve" the pain. Forgiveness just opens doors to choices and possibilities.
- **Lie no 2:** Forgiveness means we are condoning the wrong doing ... of others or ourselves. Nothing is further from the truth. Forgiving is not forgetting. We don't have recycle bins where we can throw the wrong doings. However, when you genuinely forgive, you acknowledge you have been wronged and you decide not to hold it against them. Remember what Buddha has said about anger being a hot coal you hold in your hand. So, in this case, you are throwing off the hot coal, but retaining the memory of the action, so that the next time it comes around, you can avoid the situation entirely, thus resuming the friendship without that particular conflict. The same condition

applies to yourself too. For instance, you are forgiving yourself for your procrastination, but ensure to remember how you felt while you were procrastinating, and make a conscious effort to change.

- **Lie no 3:** I am not ready. So when will you be ready? After you have lived some more years in anger and resentment? After waiting for some more years for "them" to acknowledge that they have wronged you or waiting for the person who wronged you to die? By the way, that isn't easy either; they just continue to live on in your head. That is just an excuse to stay on in the crap hole that you are in. You have a choice to move in to the clear waters of freedom and possibility. Yes, a choice.

Letting go is simpler than you think ... because forgiveness is an act of self-love. Unforgiveness creates a block in your energy system, taking away the place that could have been occupied by love, success, wealth, fame ... even freedom.

Here's your task:

Find a quiet spot. Write a letter to yourself about all the ways you have angered or disappointed yourself. Read it once. Then burn the goddamned letter (be safe, ensure you don't burn down your house!). Watch it burn, and as it burns, imagine all those emotions draining away from your body and floating away to be transmuted. Fill those empty spaces with pink light – the color of the Valentine's Day candies ... let it flood your being with mellowness, compassion and love. You are ready to step into your power.

This is a very powerful exercise. You can even write a letter to people who have hurt you and burn it. Don't mail it to them or read it to them though!

Chapter 9

I love this quote, "Happiness comes when we stop complaining about the troubles we have, and give thanks for the troubles we don't have."

First, let's finish the bad news. Life is not perfect. It never has been and never will be. Now, the good news. Once we begin to accept this reality, we welcome a great number of possibilities.

Complaining has become our go-to solution to express our pain, dissatisfaction or resentment.

Complaining keeps our focus on the negatives. And we have all heard this, "What you focus on ... grows." Complaining never results in joy – it just makes us a living, breathing 'crap' magnet. And by focusing on and drawing attention to the problems and discomforts around us, we direct other people towards it too.

So how do we shift focus? Here, I give you the promised second magic wand and its very simple: Gratitude. Peter Pan has famously said, 'All you need is a little faith, trust and pixie dust.'

Well, gratitude sprinkles that pixie dust over all your life.

Gratitude is looking for the good we already have and giving thanks ... so as you focus on what you have, it is but natural that you will have more to be thankful for!

Your question might be, "So you say. That's alright for you, but what do I have to be thankful for? I have a crappy life, my kids don't talk to me, my mother hates me, my ex-husband has remarried and moved on and I feel like a used tampon ... boohoo."

Stop! You are breathing? Great. You are alive and that's something to start with. And that is a powerful truth ... every morning, a huge chunk of people do not wake up, but you did ... so say thank you!

Kidding apart, how do we apply this in relationships, since that is at the core of our life?

Some relationships are good; some great; while some, downright crappy ... but all, I repeat, *all* of them will have something to be thankful for. As they say, you may have great experiences or great lessons ... we wouldn't be where we are in our life, if not for the relationships that propelled us here, for our growth and evolution.

True appreciation has the power to shift our focus from *what's not* to *what is.* Instead of dwelling on what a critical asshole your ex is, talk about what a great father he is. Instead of constantly complaining about how the dating scene is filled with jerks, concentrate on the great friends you found there. Be a miner, keep sifting through all that silt and sand to find the gold.

Here is an exercise that you can do to really shift the energies. I have done this successfully for over a decade now and I find it a powerful exercise. I have been accused of being too sunshiny, but that's something I can live with!

Take a blank book, I would recommend that you buy one of those expensive, good-looking notebooks – they just have a more aesthetic look, and give out a better energy, plus its motivating to write in a really good-looking book.

And every day, write down ten things to be grateful for. Now there is a format that you have to follow: You write, "I am really thankful for ____________ because I feel ___________. Thank you."

Ten things. Every day. And look for 10 different things daily. And no, you don't run out of things to be grateful for. Let's see how many I can list off the top of my head: If I start with my body, I have the air I breathe, the legs that work, the hands that can type, my skin, my smile, teeth in my mouth, my intelligence ... you get the drift. So, you have, health, money and relationships ... Conveniences – hello, even a few years ago, internet was a thing in the realm of science fiction, and what about electricity? Running water? Or even just water? You understand what I am saying? (I have a client who thanks things like the soap dish that holds the soap, the soap itself, the shampoo...everyday she finds one room to scan and say thank you!!)

Once you start being grateful for all that you have, the things you have to be grateful for just expands. Who knows what you may bring into your life, once you start vibrating at the frequency of Thankfulness.

If there is one tool that you can pick up from this book, try gratitude. It truly is magical!

Chapter 10

Questions Empower

At the end of the day, the questions we ask of ourselves determine the type of people that we will become. ~Leo Babauta

Socrates was truly the boss. He realized the power that questions have. Asking the right questions bring into your reality all that you truly desire. Now the key word here is "right." But before that, let me tell you something you may or may not know: we have a rational, logical conscious brain that controls 3% of all our activities. Yes, that's right ... it thinks it is the head (forgive the bad pun!), but only in name. The true power is in the subconscious brain, which is responsible for 97% of our thoughts, deeds and actions. Our subconscious mind is wired to find answers for whatever we ask. So if you ask questions such as "Why me?" or "Why doesn't that ever happen to me?" your brain scrambles around to figure out the answer and your subconscious mind very obligingly gives you more of the experiences to answer your 'Why.' So, you will find more and more instances to be stuck in your victim status.

Questions are powerful. I have found that just asking questions and leaving it open, unfolds a million possibilities. I want to leave you with a few questions in the area of relationships that can possibly change how you think of yourself. Just be in the question and watch what turns up for you, in your reality. Don't try to answer them; answers are conclusions that our limited understanding gives us, closing the doors on the other 999,999 possibilities.

Like the character Sara says famously in the movie, Serendipity, "You don't have to understand it; you just have to have faith."

1. What have I made so vital for not loving myself?
2. What would it change if I could honor myself for who I am?
3. What would it take for my relationships to be contributing to this world?
4. Where have I been trying too hard to harmonize my relationships?
5. What is the value of trying to fit into other people's expectations of me?
6. What is the value of always seeking approval in my relationships?
7. What if I could be myself and still create a beautiful relationship with everyone?
8. How much power am I giving away by choosing to live in my past?
9. What energy, space and consciousness should I and my body be in order to create harmony within and around me?
10. What's right about me that I am not getting?
11. Am I willing to be different enough to create a relationship? If I were to be truly me, who would I be waiting for?
12. And what am I using as a justification for not having the life and the relationship that I desire?

Afterword

It has been a long journey for me, to live the way that I am living, where I feel totally at peace and not in any need to resist, react, agree or align with anything. It has not been easy. And when you are living your life challenges, there are times when you fall off the Pollyanna wagon and slip in to a victim or orphan mode. That is where like-minded friends support you. The people you associate with, will truly determine the level of your success.

What have I taught my children?

I hope when they look at me, they know that Love is really what makes our world go round ... and that love starts with ourselves, because we can only attract that which we already have within us.

I hope they have learned to trust themselves and their intuitions.

I hope they have learned to lead with their heart.

I hope they have learned to say *no* when they mean no.

I hope they have learned to speak up when they needed to and speak out when required.

I hope they have learned that it is great to shine their brilliance, because somehow it may inspire someone else to do the same.

I hope they have learned that the prince and princess both reside within themselves, and when they are whole and complete, they will attract mates who are whole and complete within themselves too … and together, they grow and contribute to the greater consciousness of this world. Because tomorrow really belongs to them.

www.ingramcontent.com/pod-product-compliance
Lightning Source LLC
La Vergne TN
LVHW090317160826
845684LV00001B/4
* 9 7 9 8 8 9 5 1 9 0 5 9 3 *